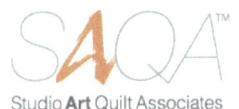

I0390499

Natural Healing

An exhibit of contemporary fiber art

Presented by Studio Art Quilt Associates of New Mexico

2015-2016

Since the dawn of history, humans have used plants and animals to cure the sick, heal wounds, and promote health. Our challenge for Natural Healing was to create a representation, in a 20x30" piece of fiber art, of one or more plants or animals that contribute to human wellness. Inspiration could be from ancient or cutting edge medicine.

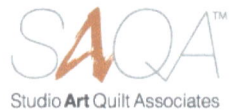

Exhibition Schedule

2015
First Unitarian Church, Albuquerque, NM, October 11-November 20, 2015

2016
- Hubbard Museum of the American West, Ruidoso Downs, NM
- National Institutes of Health, Bethesda, MD
- Inova Cancer Center, Fair Oaks Hospital, Fairfax, VA
- University of Michigan Health System, Ann Arbor, MI

For an updated list of exhibit locations, visit HealingQuiltsinMedicine.org

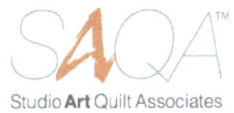

Who are we?

SAQA is an international organization that promotes quilting as an art form and serves to educate the public about the history of quilts and their significance in contemporary art. The exhibition is open to fiber artists who are members of the New Mexico region of SAQA.

Contemporary art quilts are part of a revolutionary movement that has transcended the once strict barriers between the craft of quilting and fine art, filling a niche somewhere between sculpture and painting. These artists combine their exceptional skills in working with fabrics, threads, and their artistic insights to craft stunning tactile creations that inspire, elevate, and encourage reflection.

To learn more, visit www.saqa.com

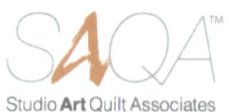

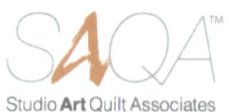

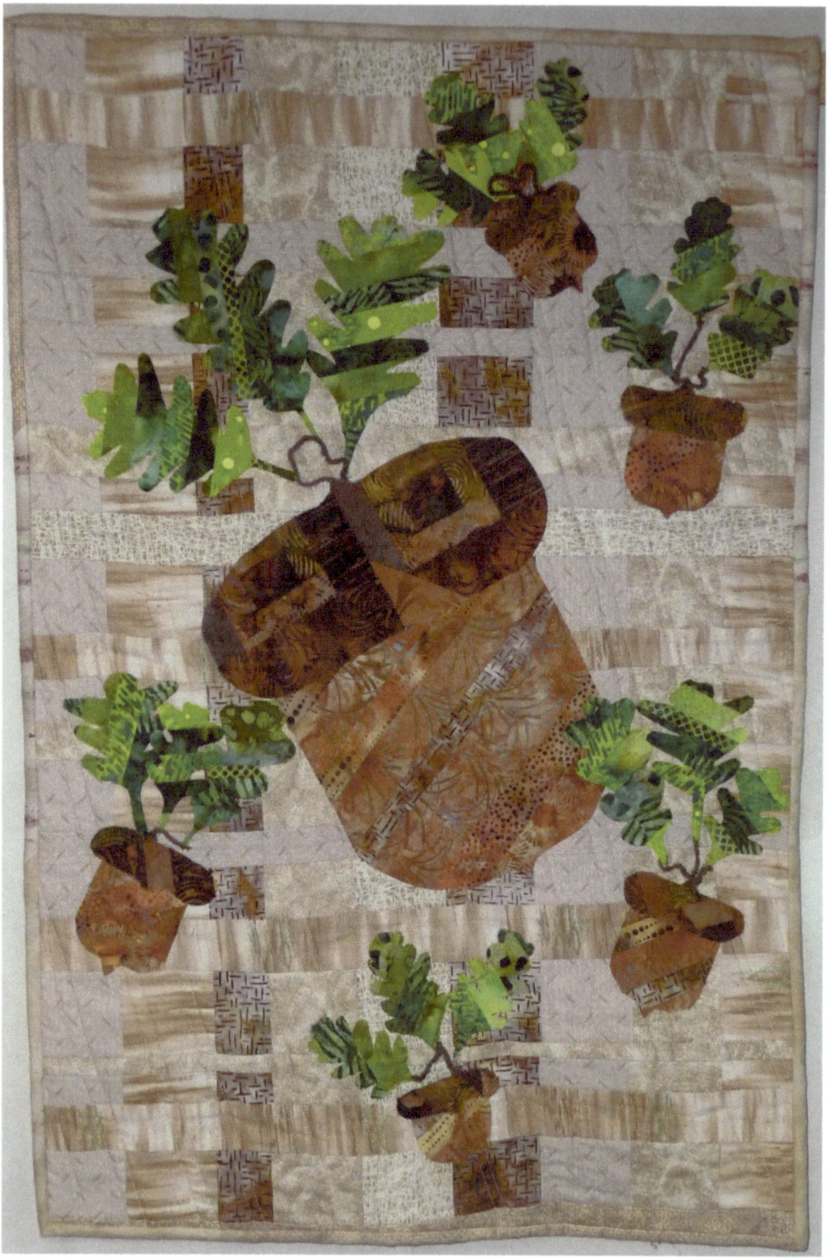

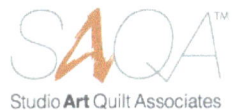

Ann Anastasio, Santa Fe, NM
aanastasio@comcast.net

Oak Leaves and Acorns

Native Americans used ground oak leaves to heal wounds and they also used ground acorns mixed with other natural materials for headaches and minor pain. With commercial fabrics, I machine pieced the background, acorns and leaves using different random piecing designs for each shape. The background is diagonally machine quilted.

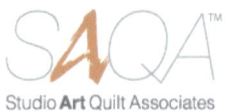

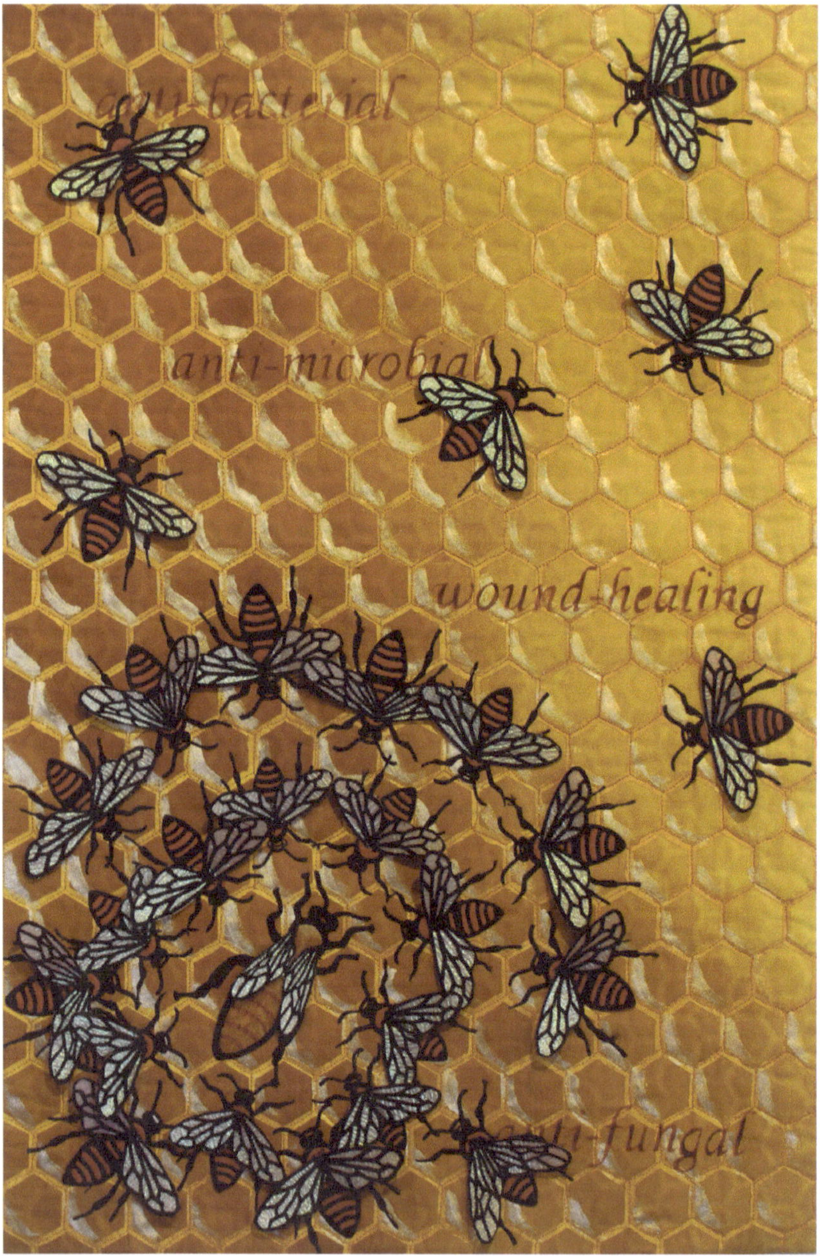

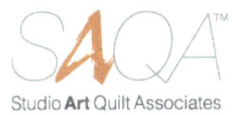

Schatzi Brimer, Santa Fe, NM

sbrimerartquilts@gmail.com

Honey, the Golden Elixir

Honey has been called "Liquid Gold", the "Nectar of the Gods" and "the Golden Elixir" and for good reason. Since ancient times, honey was used for medicinal purposes. As early as 2100 BC, honey's use as an ointment and drug was recorded. Aristotle (384-322 BC) referred to honey as being a good salve for sore eyes and wounds. Today, honey is known to possess antimicrobial properties and aides in wound healing. It is thought that honey also demonstrates anti-bacterial properties against antibiotic-resistant bacteria. Honey may also suppress coughs, soothe burns, act as a sleep aid, boost immunity, treat dandruff and has anti-fungal properties. A remarkable substance, and it tastes good too! How sweet is that?

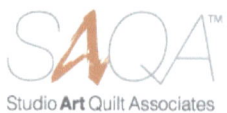

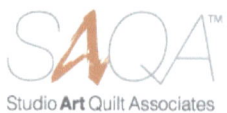

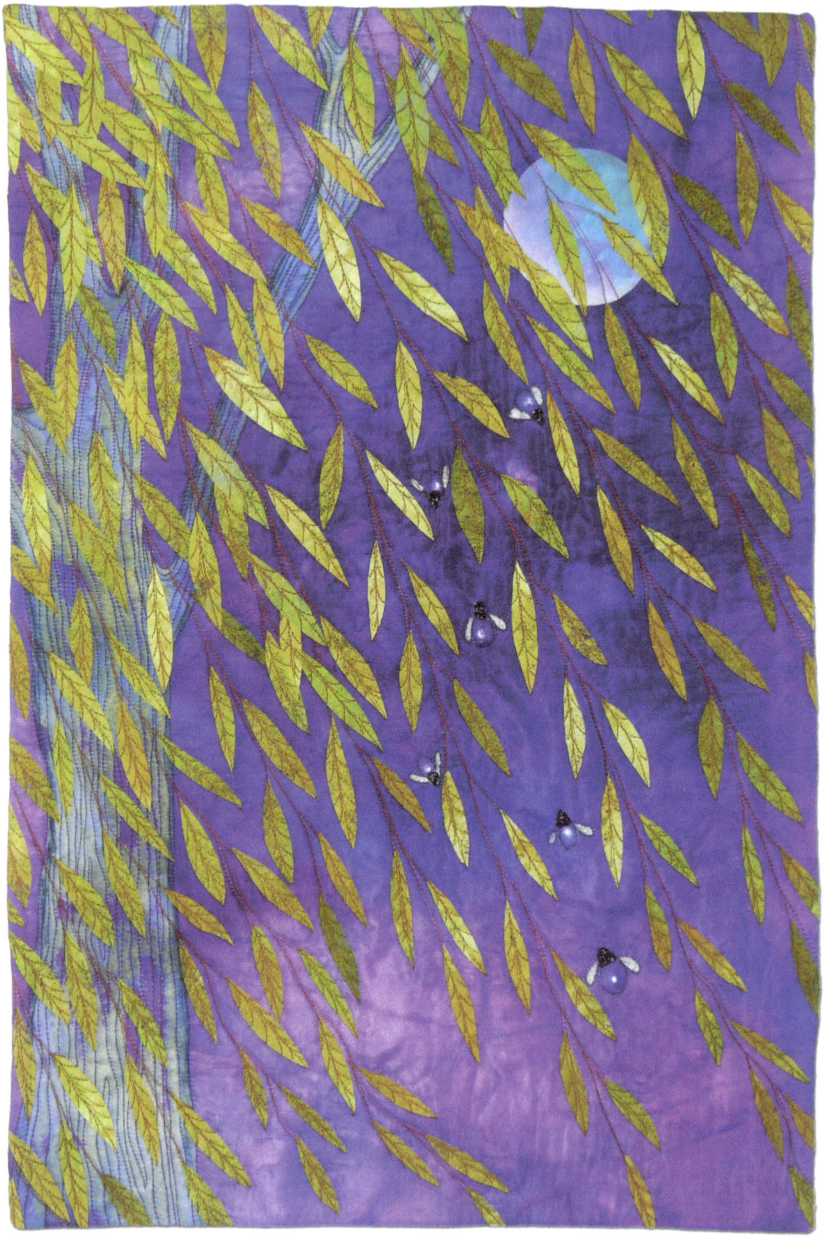

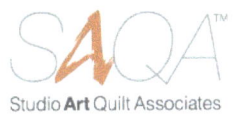

Betty Busby, Albuquerque NM
fbusby3@comcast.net
bbusbyarts.com

Salix

The use of willow bark dates back thousands of years, to the time of Hippocrates (400 BC) when patients were advised to chew on the bark to reduce fever and inflammation. Willow bark has been used throughout the centuries in China and Europe, and continues to be used today for the treatment of pain.

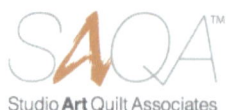

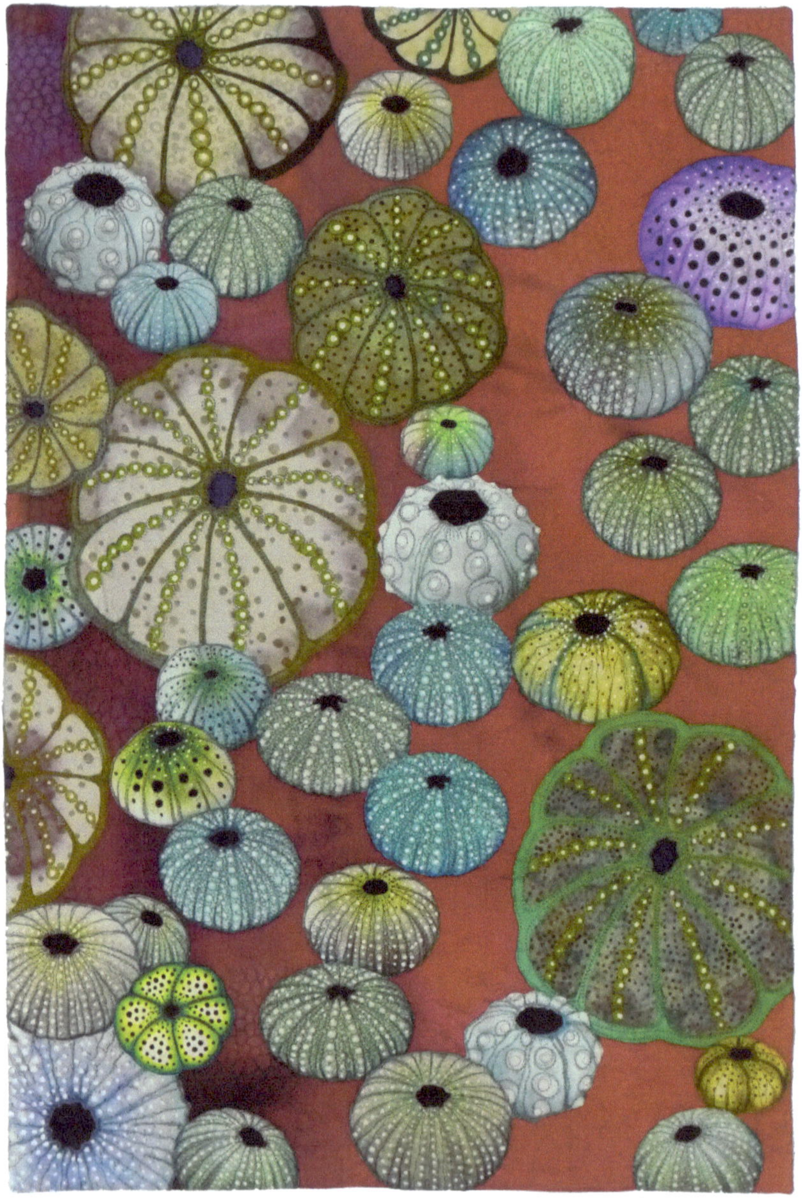

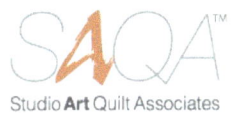

Betty Busby, Albuquerque NM
fbusby3@comcast.net
bbusbyarts.com

Sea Urchin: SpTransformer

Sea urchins contain immune proteins with anti microbial functions. Bonnie Lun is focusing her doctoral research on one that she has renamed SpTransformer. This compound, part of the ShapeShifter group, will have profound beneficial effects in future medicine.

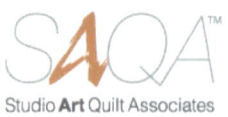

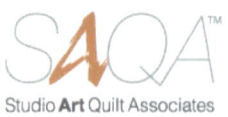

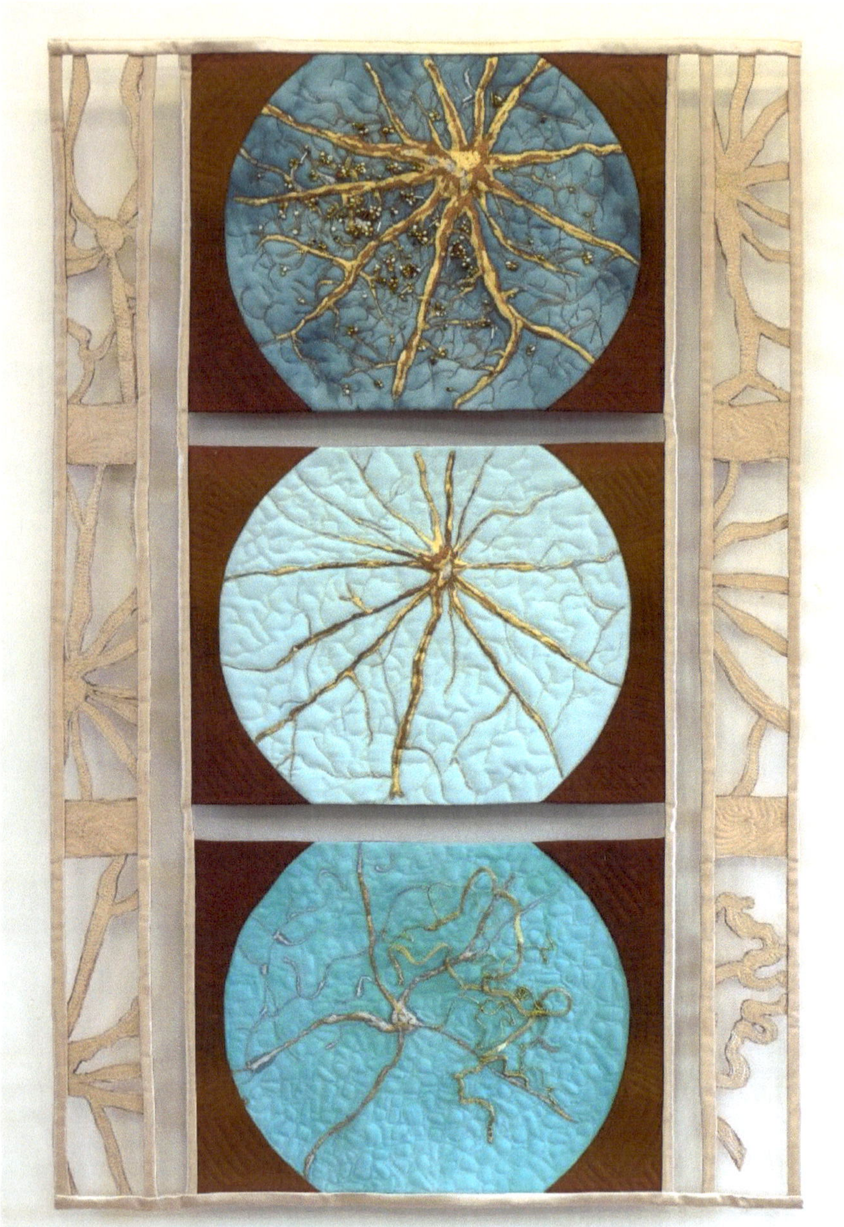

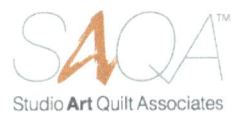

Shannon M. Conley, Moore, OK
la.emperatriz@gmail.com
shannonconleyartquilts.com

Two Blind Mice and a Wild-Type

Knockout and knockin mice are genetically engineered to carry mutations in their genome to model debilitating diseases, critical since it is difficult to study many diseases in human patients. The scientific and medical advancements that have resulted from use of these models cannot be overstated. This quilt re-interprets my fluorescein angiograms -- pictures of the blood vessels in the eye -- from mice with diabetic retinopathy (top) and macular dystrophy (bottom), as well as their normal or wild type counterpart (middle). We use these specialized mice to study the pathobiological mechanisms associated with these blinding retinal degenerations and to develop and test novel treatments.

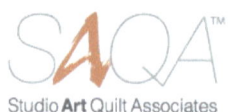

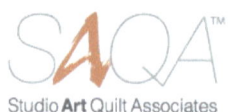

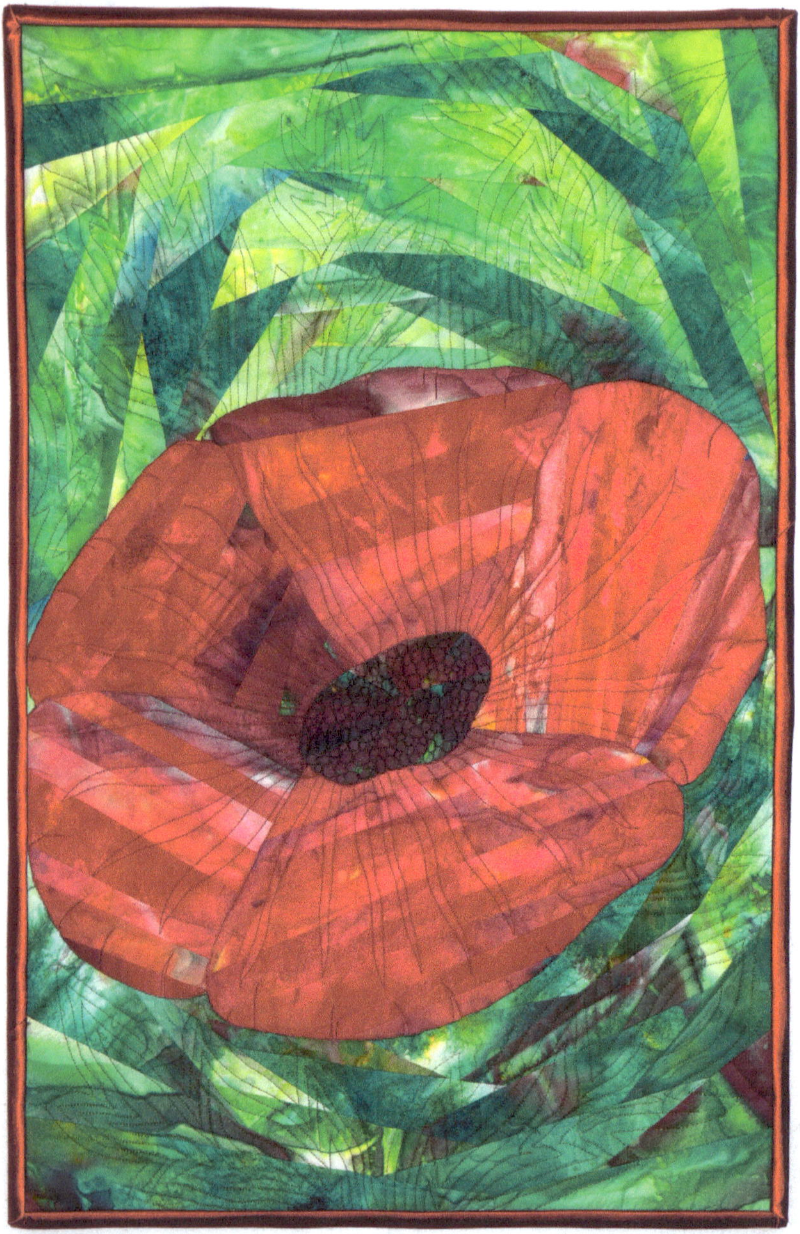

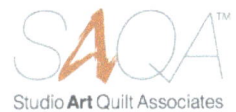

Vicki Conley, Ruidoso Downs, NM

vicki1onley@yahoo.com

vicki-conley.com

Flanders Poppy

The unwarranted invasion of neutral Belgium became a rallying point for allied forces in the early days of the First World War. The poppy fields of Flanders (in northern Belgium) were one of the most visually striking sites of the demoralizing and interminable trench warfare which characterized the conflict and during which so many soldiers gave their lives. Ever since then, the poppy has been given out as a remembrance of fallen service members. This outward and visible symbol helps us cope with the sacrifice others have made and helps to heal our spirit.

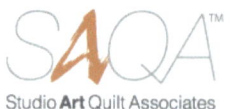

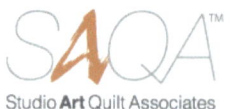

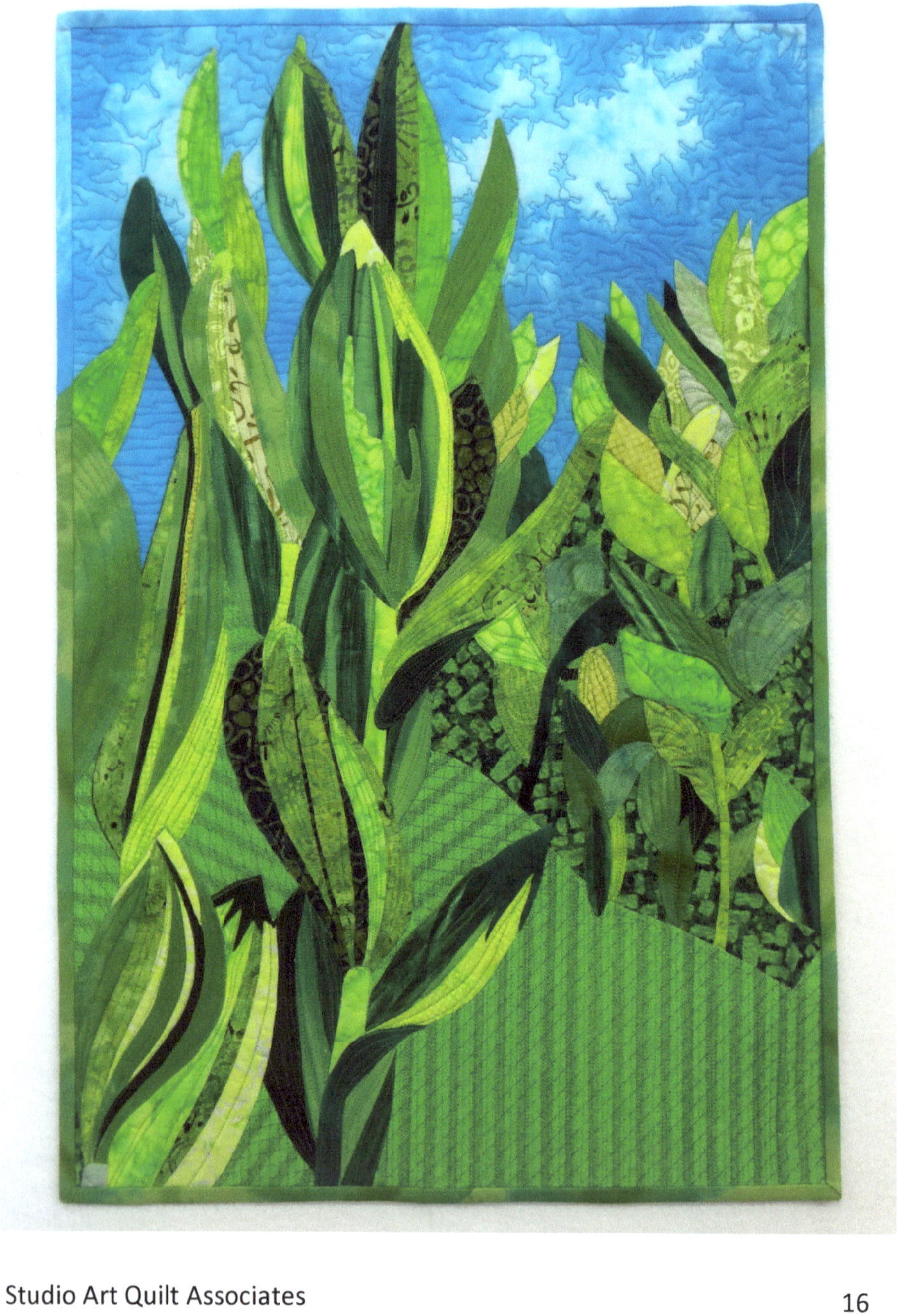

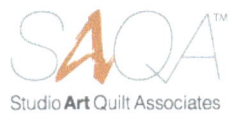

Nicole Dunn, Los Alamos, NM
nicole@dunnassoc.net, dunnquilting.com

Corn Lily

Veratrum californicum, also known as Corn Lily or False Hellebore is a poisonous plant native to mountain meadows of North America. However, in researching this amazing plant, I found out that its flower essence has been used to help with symptoms of menopause in women by practitioners in Mexico. Also, a derivative of the plant, called Cyclopamine, is currently undergoing clinical trials for treatment of hard to treat cancers such as hematologic malignancies, chondrosarcoma, and pancreatic cancer.

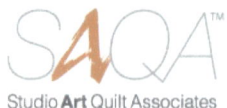

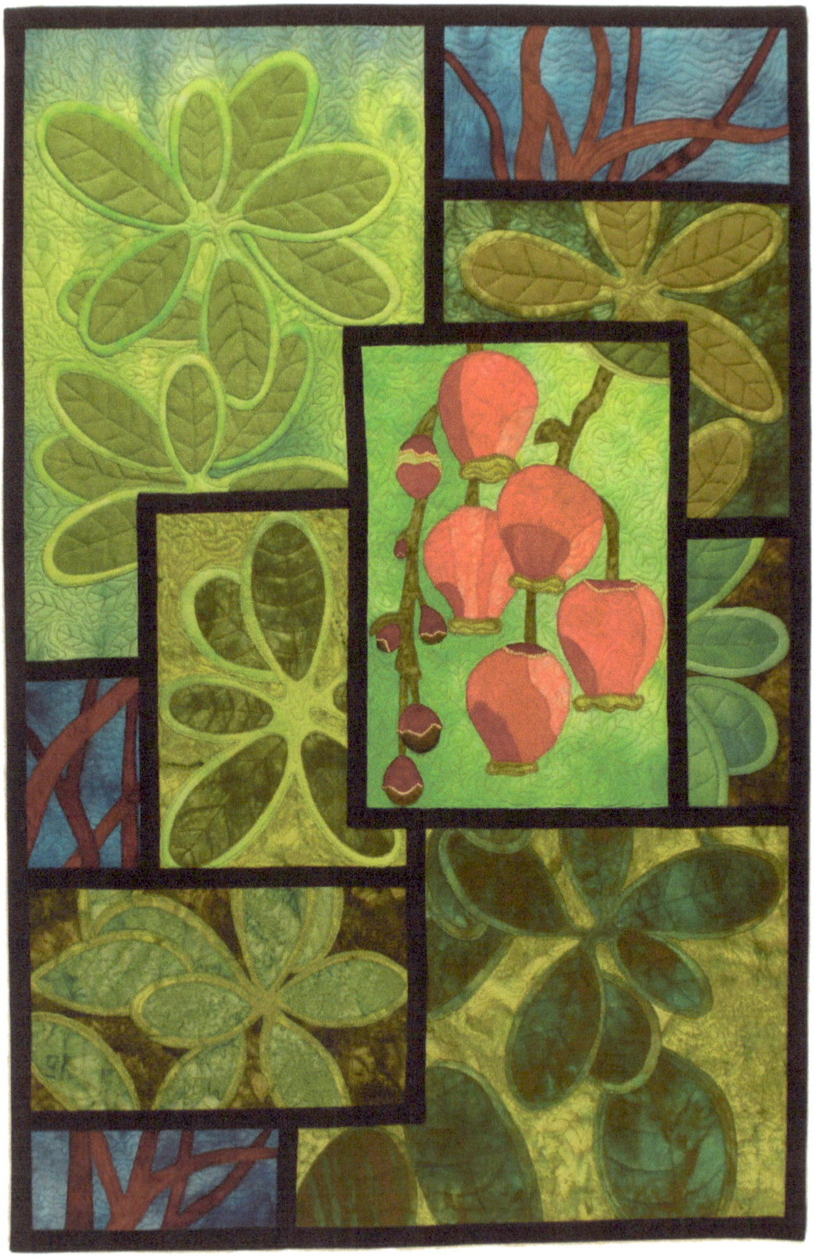

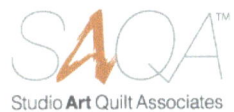

Cheryl FitzGerald, Albuquerque, NM
cherylf@swcp.com
cherylfquilts.com

Manzanita

Manzanita is a common name for a small tree or shrub found in western United States that has been used by traditional healers, most commonly for urinary tract infections and treatment of poison oak rash. It is a Spanish word that translates as "little apple" for its small reddish berries, which ripen in late summer. In this quilt I wanted to focus on its characteristic berries, leaves, and twisting branches.

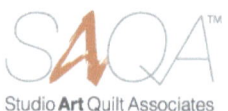

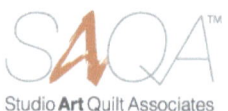

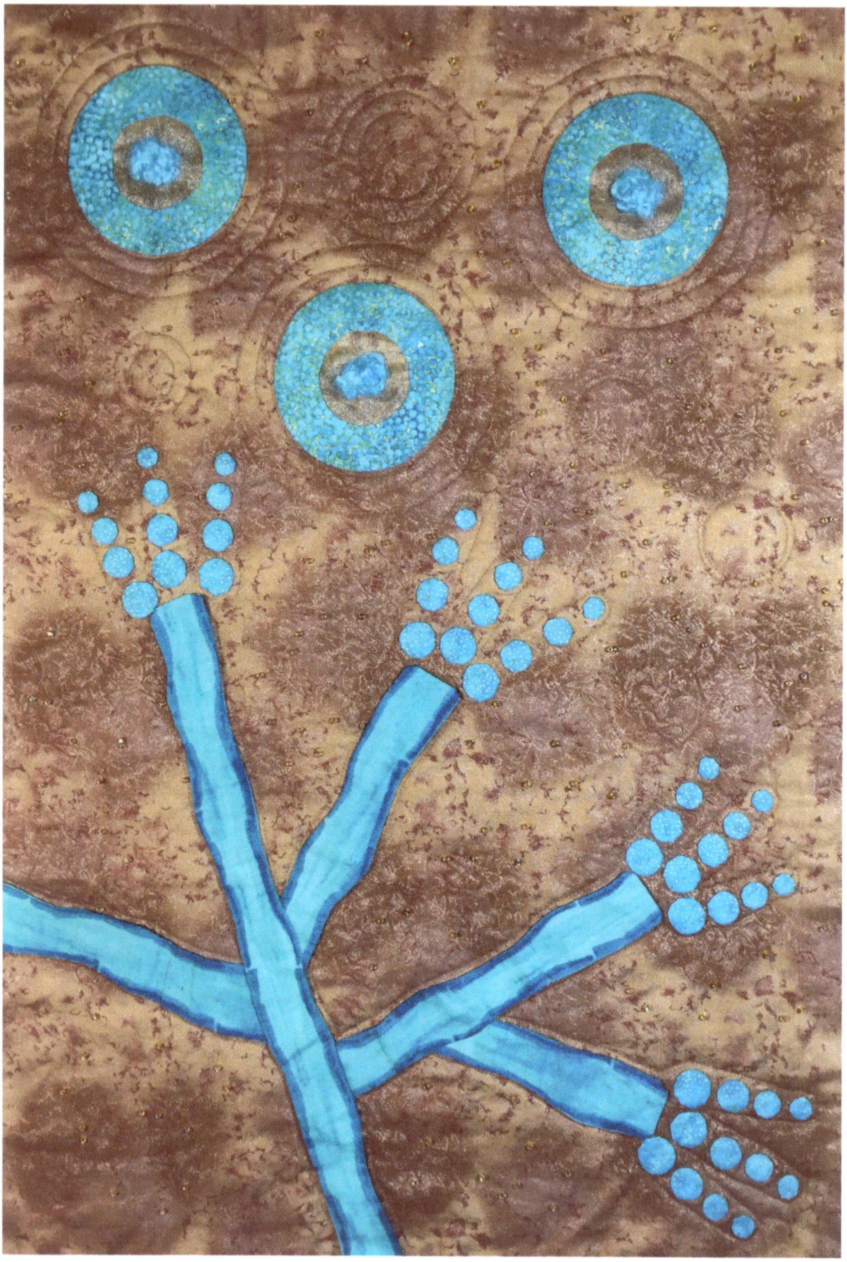

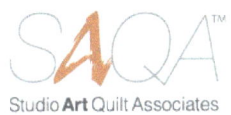

Cynthia Fowler, Santa Fe, NM
melifowl@yahoo.com

Penicillium

There was a time when a simple cut finger could result in loss of limb and life. Everyone viewing this quilt has in some way been affected by the discovery of penicillin in 1928 and the plethora of anti-microbial agents that followed. The discovery of penicillin from the mold *Penicillium*, ushered in a new age of antibiotics derived from microorganisms and marked a true turning point in human history: doctors finally had a tool that could completely cure their patients of deadly infectious diseases. Penicillin was like magic. It was so precious, that syringes were reused without washing in between doses. No one wanted to waste a drop of this "liquid gold". Like so many scientific advances, the discovery of penicillin was due to serendipity and the curiosity of a scientist, Alexander Fleming. Subsequently Howard Florey, Norman Heatley, and Ernst Chain developed methods for manufacture and application in humans that resulted in the ability to mass-produce penicillin in quantities great enough for distribution and mass use in combat troops during WWII.

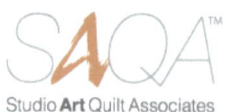

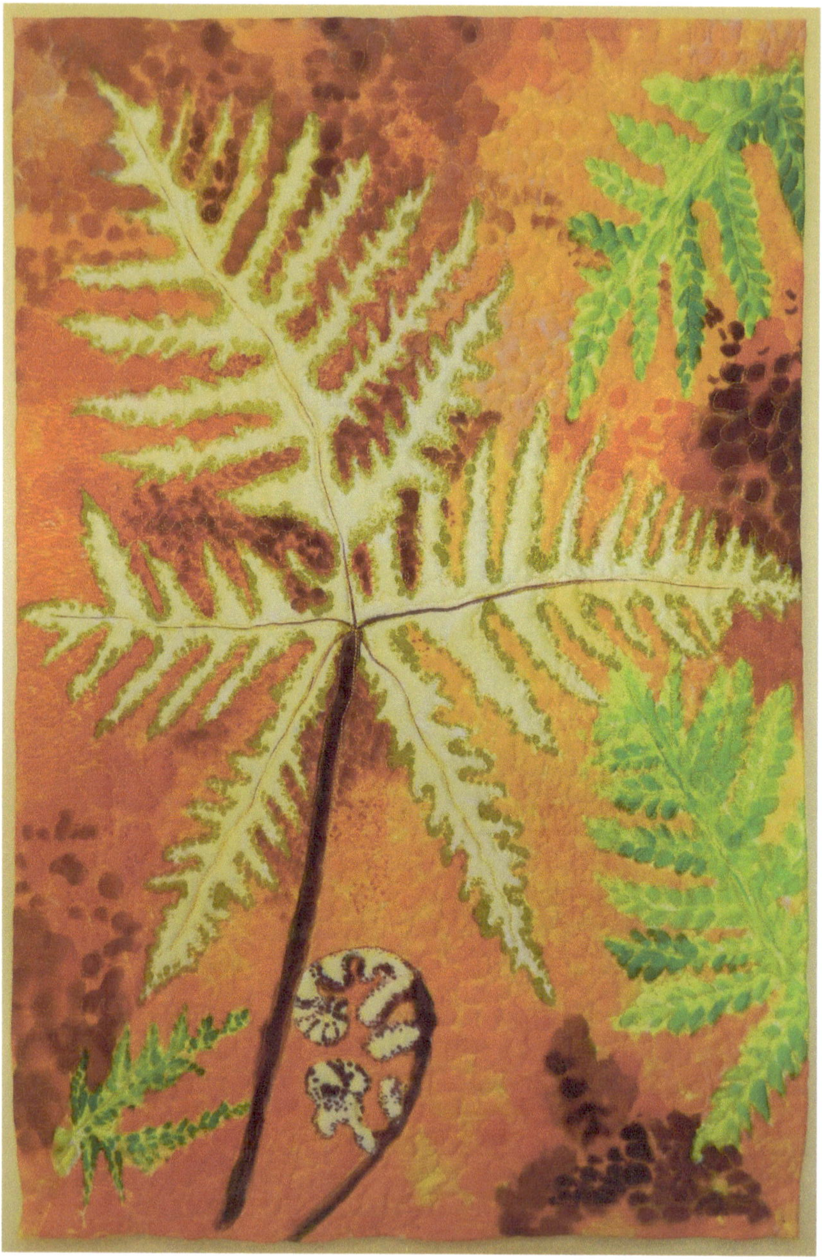

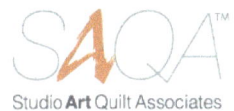
Betty Hahn, Sun City, AZ
bghahb49@aol.com
bettyhahnfiberart.blogspot.com

Standley's Cloak Fern

While in New Mexico I met a young man who works for the Forest Service. I asked him if there was a plant mostly grown in the Southwest United States that was used for medicinal purposes. He stated that there was a fern with a pentagonal leaf shape that was used by the Seri Indians for fertility. He called it a cloak fern. I discovered the fern grows here in my area in the Phoenix mountain preserve and across Arizona, New Mexico and Mexico. It is called *Notholaena standleyi* and was used by the Seri Indians as a fertility aid and for general good fortune. It is now used in the treatment of Herpes virus. It can be found nestled in cracks of granite rocks. The front is green and the back is light yellow with a border of greenish yellow. When faced with drought conditions it curls up to protect itself.

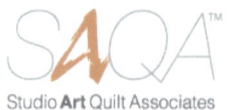

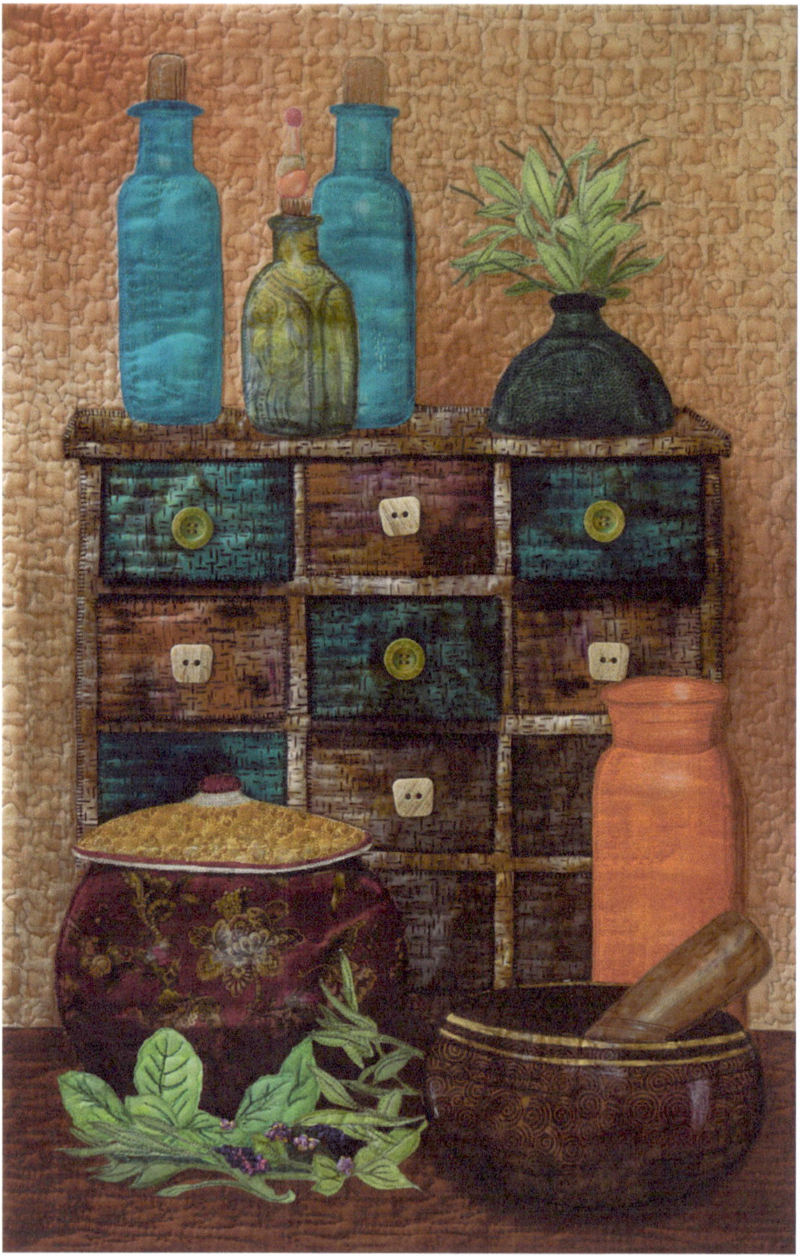

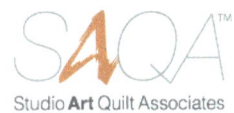

Lorraine Hollingsworth, Albuquerque, NM

laholli@live.com

The Apothecary

Historically, an apothecary was a person who prepared and sold materia medica to physicians, surgeons and patients. They were an important part of European and Colonial towns and cities. Some eighteenth century apothecaries also practiced as doctors or physicians. The apothecary started out in the 14th century as a seller of spices and drugs. Today, there are still apothecaries that specialize in herbal and other natural products, some of which have been in operation for hundreds of years.

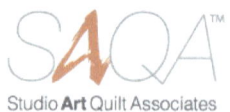

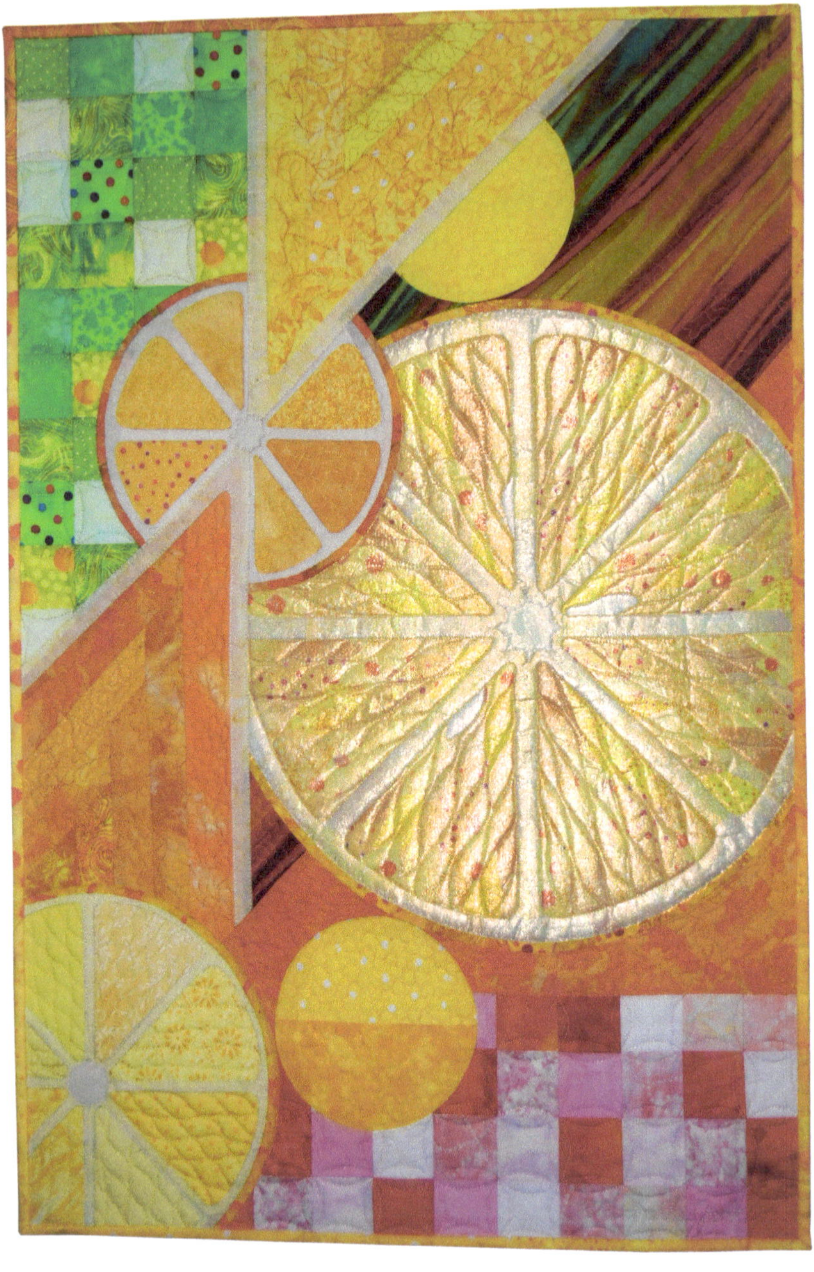

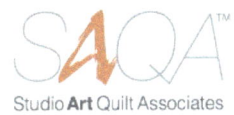

Michelle M. Jackson
Albuquerque, NM
michellejackson@quiltfashions.com
www.quiltfashions.com

Lemon Squeeze

Lemons have strong antibacterial, antiviral, and immune-boosting powers. They contain citric acid, calcium, magnesium, vitamin C, bioflavonoids, pectin, and limonene that promote immunity and fight infection.

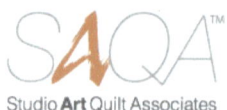

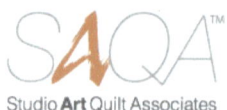

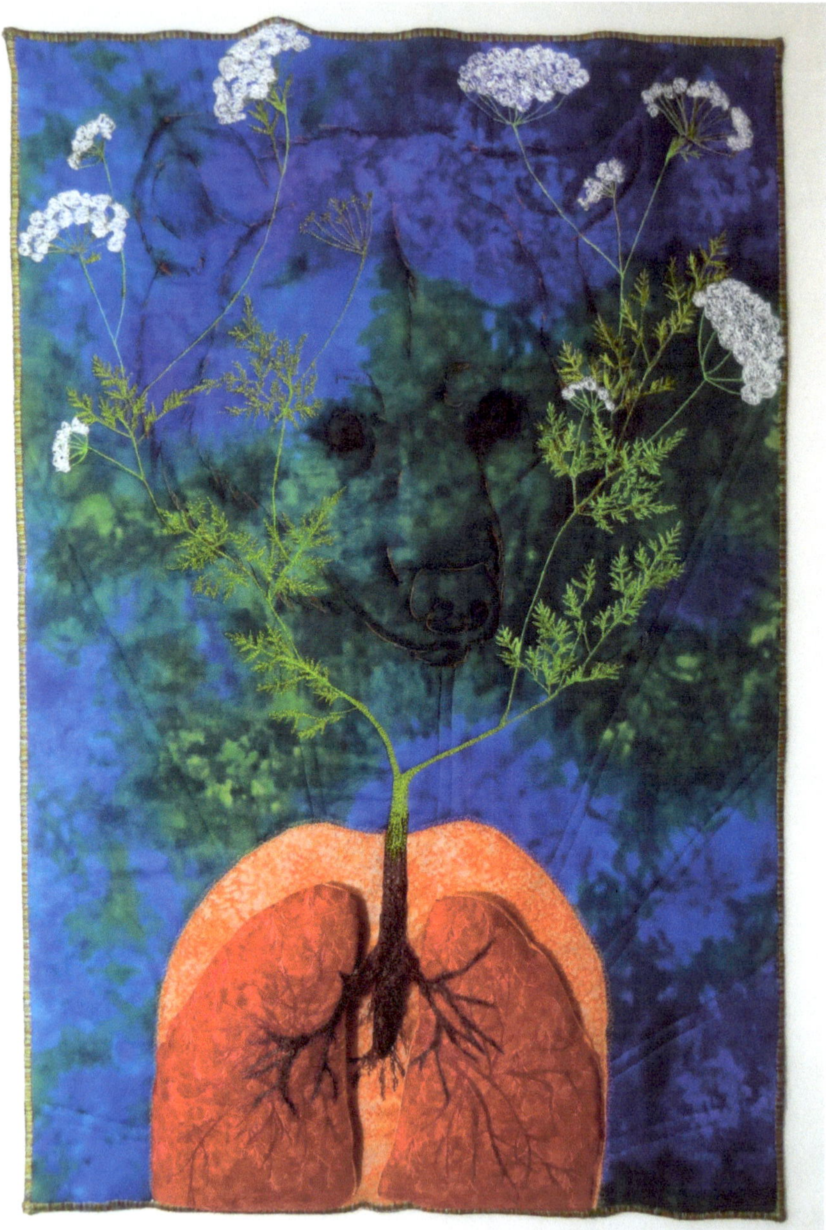

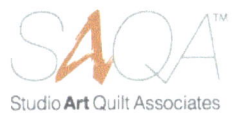
Ginny McVickar, Pleasant Hill, OR
mcvickarg@gmail.com

OSHA - The Bear Plant

Osha, (*Ligusticum porteri*) or Chuchupate, also called bear root, is a perennial herb that inhabits the Rocky Mountain Region above 9,000 feet. The beneficial part of the Osha plant is the root, which has long been used by Native Americans for cold, cough, and other respiratory ailments. Osha root is, arguably, the best American herb for lung and throat problems. Bears would look for Osha and consume the plant roots directly after emerging from winter hibernation or when wounded or sick.

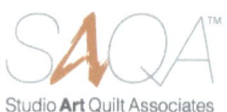

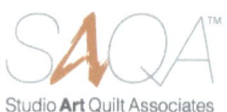

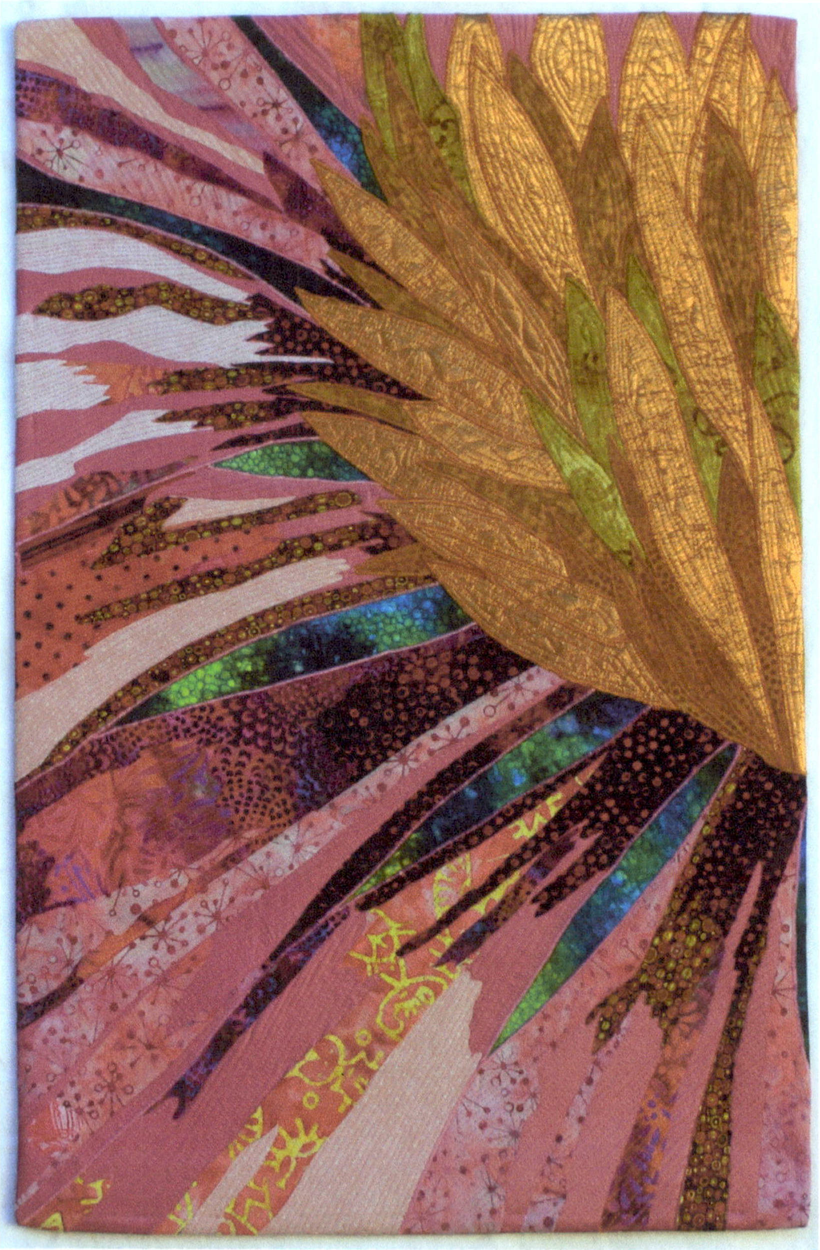

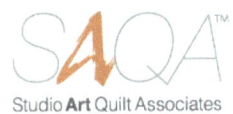

Frances Oldham Murphy, Surprise, AZ
francesmurphy50@msn.com

Maxima (*Echinacea purpurea*)

I have always been fascinated by the Echinacea flower. I love the contrast between the floppy pinkish-purple leaves and the spiky red- gold center. When I look back through the photographs, sketchbooks, and "doodles" I have accumulated throughout my life, I find the Echinacea flower in abundance. As a natural remedy, Echinacea stimulates the immune system and is said to shorten the duration of the common cold.

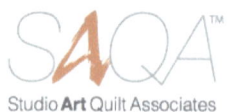

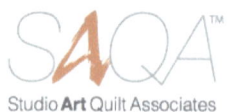

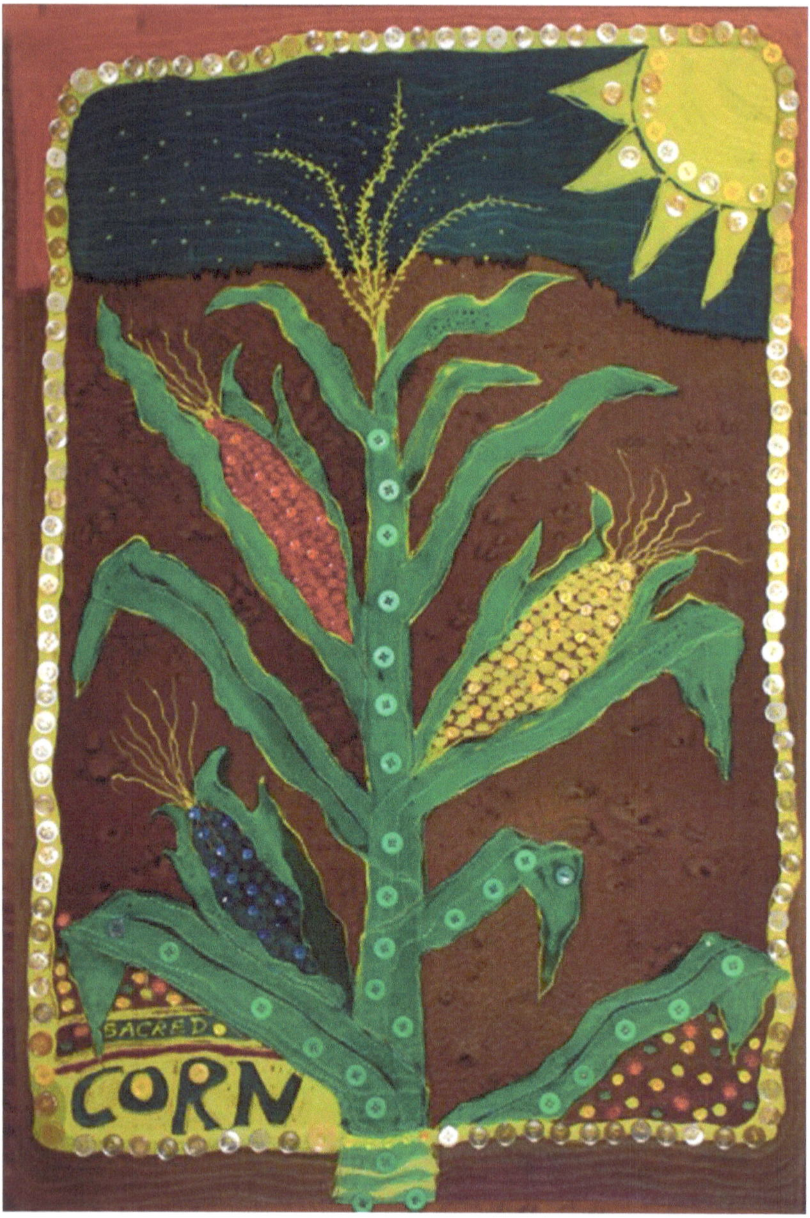

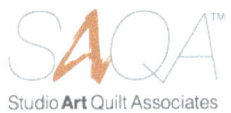

Judith Roderick, Placitas, NM

rainbowpaintr@comcast.net

Sacred Corn

Corn has been a sacred plant to many indigenous peoples of the Americas for millennia. Mayans, Aztecs, and many Native American peoples worshipped Corn Gods and developed myths about the origin, planting, growing, and harvesting of corn. Corn appeared in their Creation Stories, as the Source of Creation, as a Corn Gods and Goddesses, as medicine and food for the people. Corn dances are still performed each year in the Southwest. The pollen is sacred and the corn silk has been used as medicine. Corn is one of the three sisters, with beans and squash, and has been important nourishment in the Southwest, eaten fresh, dried and ground into cornmeal. Cornmeal is also used as an offering. This quilt depicts the red, yellow and blue corn, the corn silk and the pollen. It is whole cloth hand-painted silk, machine quilted, with hand-sewn buttons.

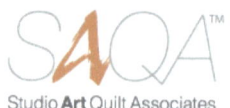

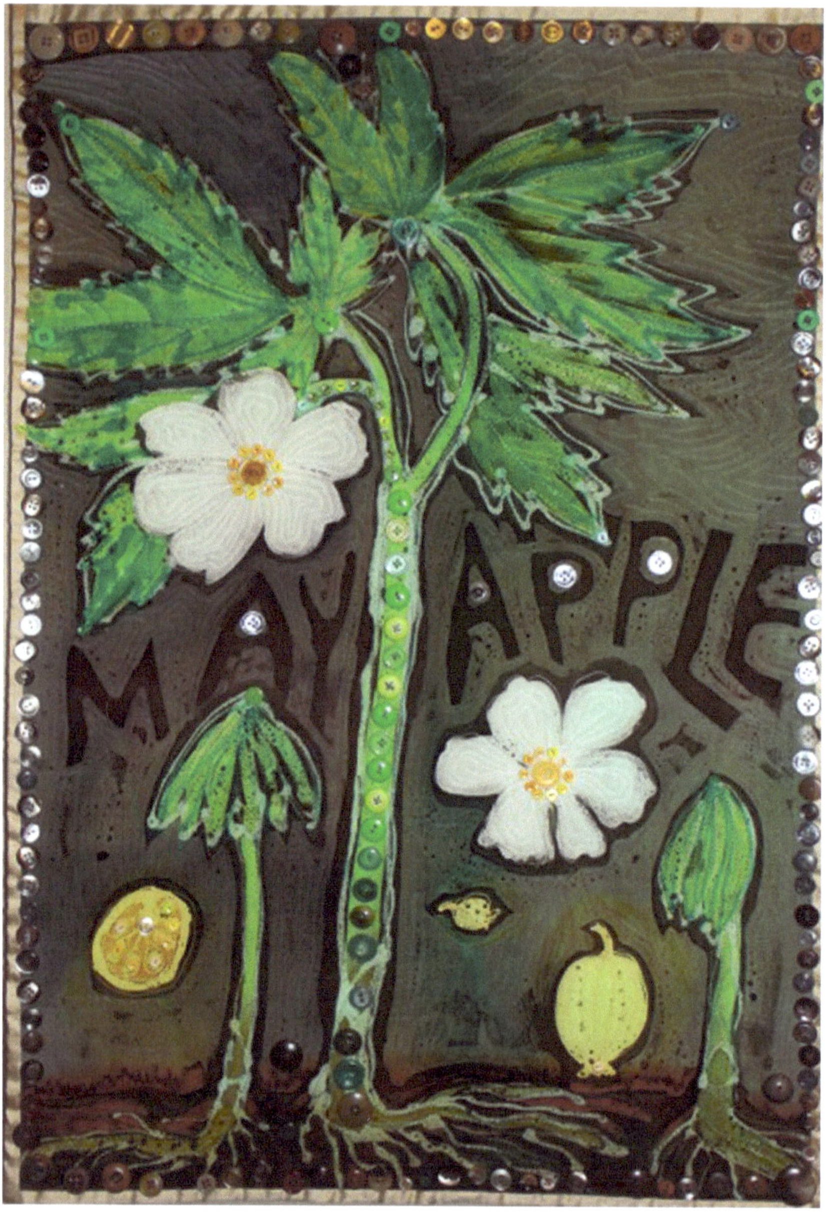

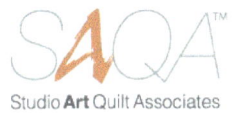

Judith Roderick, Placitas, NM
rainbowpaintr@comcast.net

May Apple, American Mandrake,
(*Podophyllum peltatum*)

This is a nostalgia quilt for me, as I fondly remember a carpet of May apples emerging in the early Spring in the woods near my home in Western Pennsylvania, when I was growing up. I always enjoyed their umbrella-like leaves and lovely white flowers. Native American tribes used their dried and powdered root as a laxative, to remove worms, and as a topical treatment for skin cancer. They often ate the ripened fruit also. Modern medicine has found compounds in the root, or rhizome that contain valuable constituents such as quercetin that are being studied for their healing anti-cancer properties. This is a whole-cloth, hand-painted silk quilt, that was machine quilted and embellished with hand-sewn buttons.

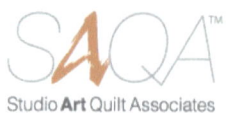

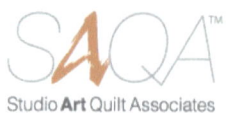

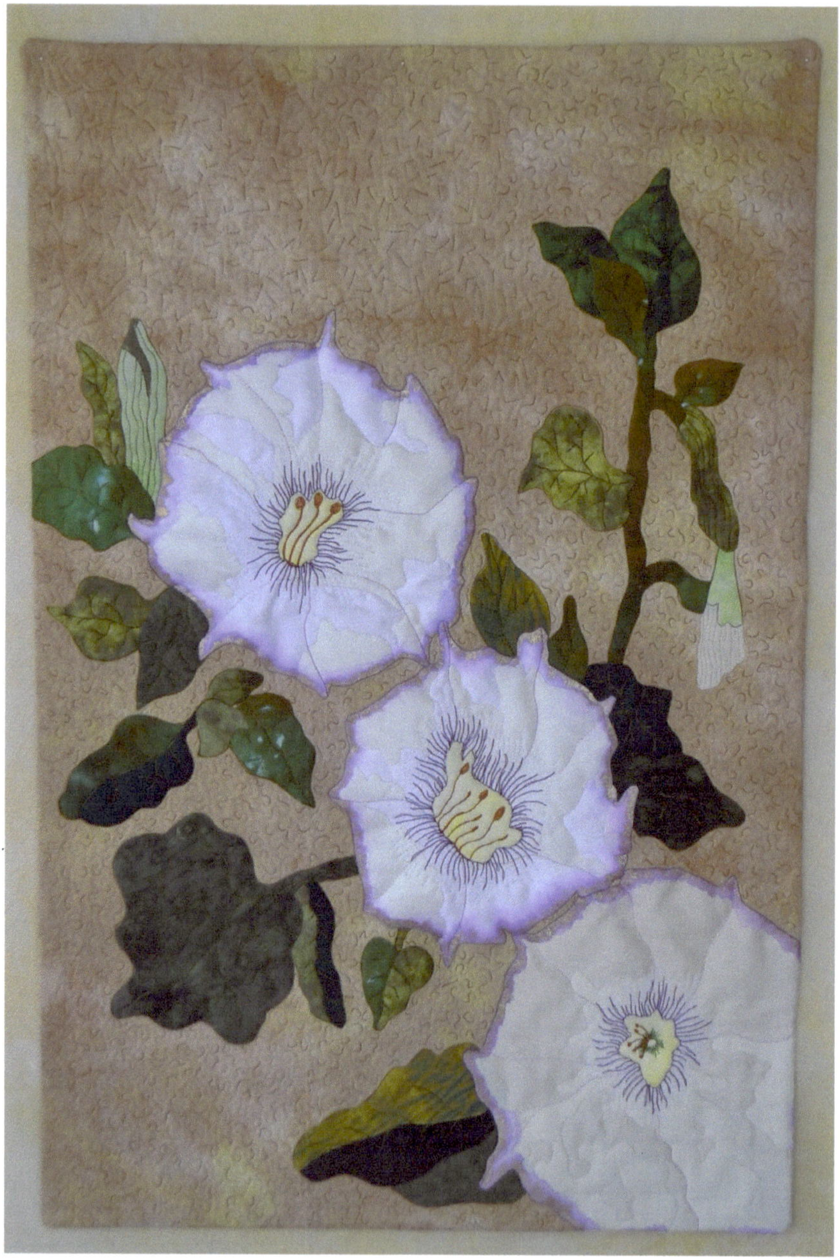

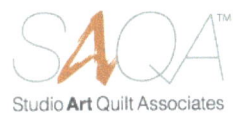

Lynn Rogers, Rio Ranch, NM
kblr049@aol.com

Sacred Datura (*Datura meteloides*)

Known by other names such as moonflower or Jimson weed, Sacred Datura is a beautiful plant with large, white flowers, made famous in paintings by Georgia O'Keefe. It is native to the Four Corners region of the United States, Texas, California and south into Mexico. The Aztecs made a poultice for wounds from this plant, but most often it is known as an entheogen, which is a plant that is ingested to induce hallucinogenic effects for religious or spiritual purposes. Large variations exist from plant to plant, and a given plant's toxicity depends on its age, where it is growing and the local weather conditions. These variables make it exceptionally hazardous to use as a drug. In traditional cultures, users needed to have a great deal of experience and detailed plant knowledge so that no harm resulted from its use.

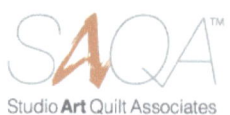

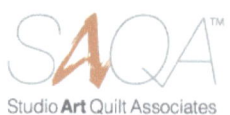

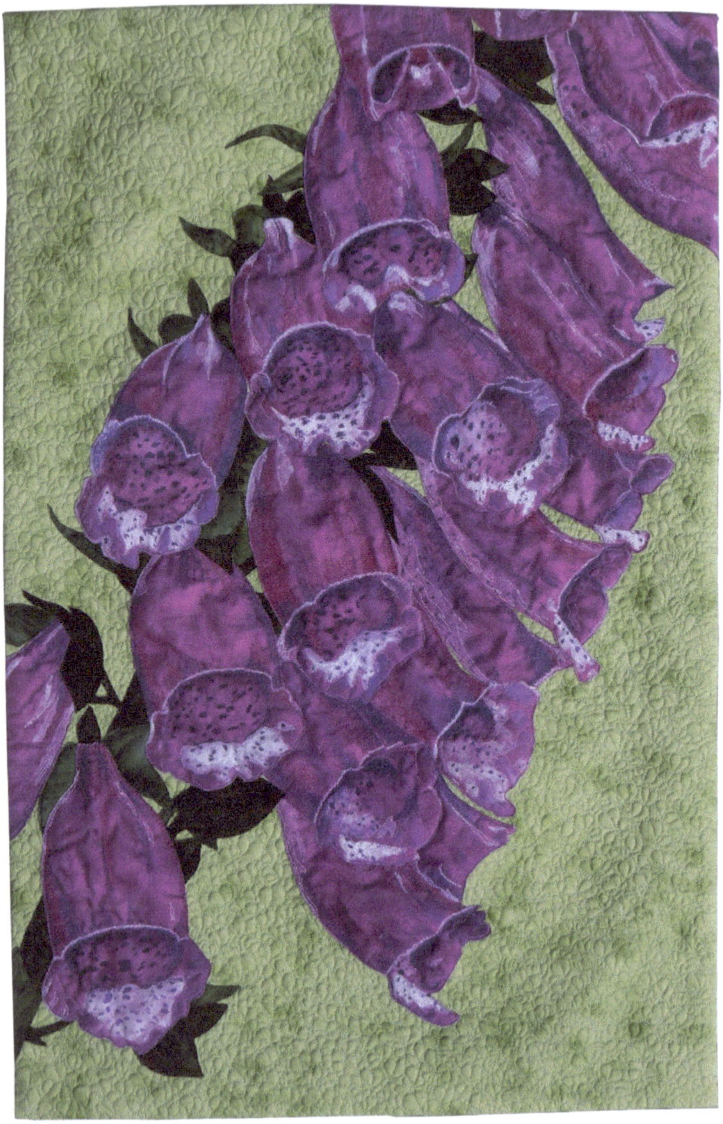

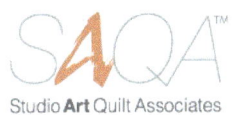

Denise Seavey, Santa Fe, NM

den@insiteworks.com

Foxglove (*Digitalis purpurea*)

Foxglove has been used in the treatment of heart conditions since 1785. Digitalis, a derivative of Foxglove may be prescribed for patients with atrial fibrillation. Strolling through Europe this past summer, I was fortunate to see this magnificent flower. Materials used include acrylic paint, batiks and cottons.

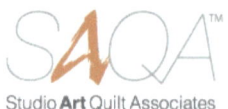

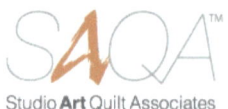

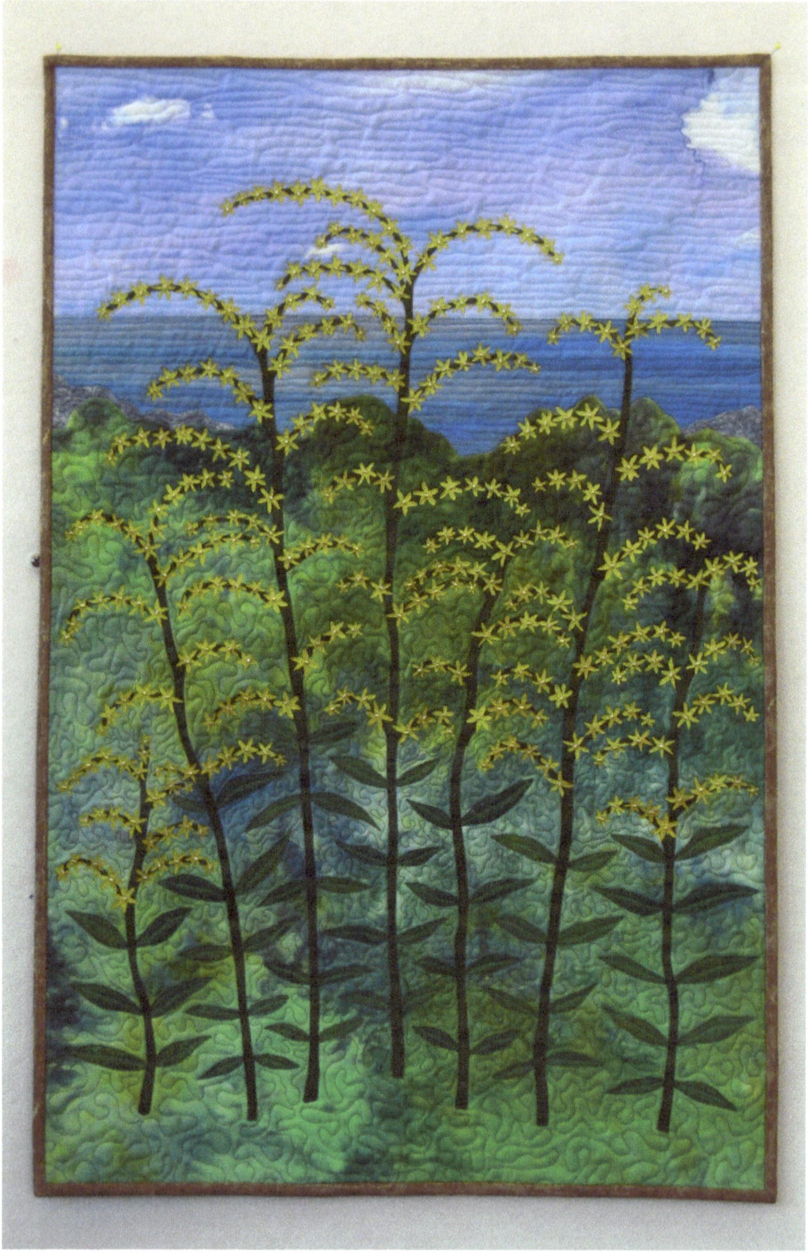

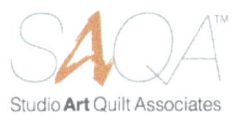

Lynn B. Welsch, Mimbres, NM
lbwelsch@hughes.net

Monhegan Island Goldenrod

Goldenrod is used around the world to treat tuberculosis, diabetes, enlargement of the liver, gout, hemorrhoids, internal bleeding, asthma, arthritis, inflammation, muscle spasms, infections, and blood pressure. It acts as a diuretic and is used in teas to "flush out" or treat and prevent kidney stones. Goldenrod is often blamed for seasonal allergies when Ragweed, which blooms at the same time, is responsible!

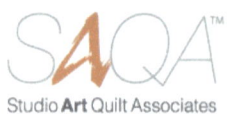

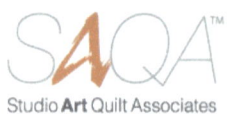

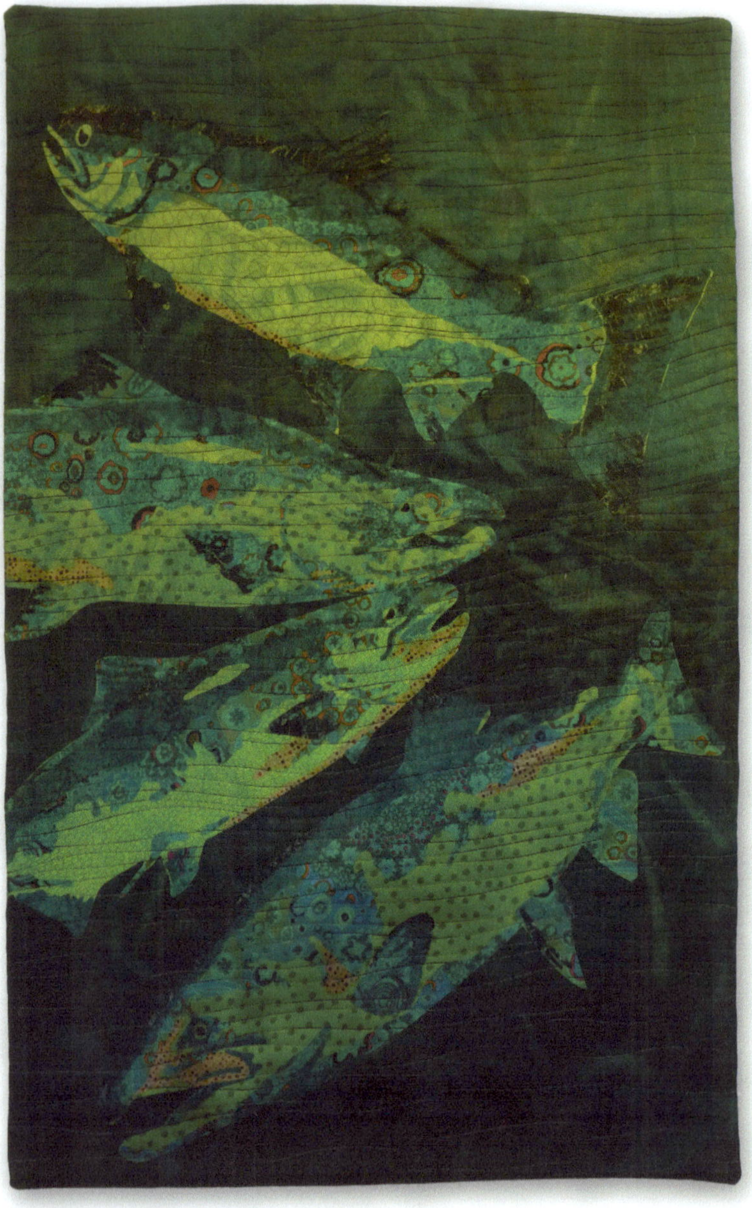

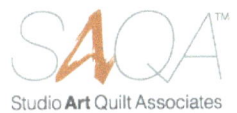

Martha Wolfe, Davis, CA
mwfiberart@me.com

Chinook

Chinook Salmon have played an important role in medicine in Native People's history, in totem images symbolizing health and stories that remind us that nature is our first source for healing. Today, modern pharmacology recognizes the valuable "medicines" provided by salmon. A rich source of vitamin D and calcium, salmon promotes bone health, as well as helping control blood sugar and boost immunity. The omega-3 fatty acids, DHA and EPA may reduce inflammation and the risk of heart disease, improve cognitive function, enhance fetal development, and a host of other benefits.

www.ingramcontent.com/pod-product-compliance
Lightning Source LLC
Chambersburg PA
CBHW041208180526
45172CB00006B/1217